D1533129

THE AMERICAN POETRY REVIEW/HONICKMAN FIRST BOOK PRIZE

The Honickman Foundation is dedicated to the support of projects that promote spiritual growth and creativity, education and social change. At the heart of the mission of the Honickman Foundation is the belief that creativity enriches contemporary society because the arts are powerful tools for enlightenment, equity and empowerment, and must be encouraged to effect social change as well as personal growth. A current focus is on the particular power of photography and poetry to reflect and interpret reality, and, hence, to illuminate all that is true.

The annual American Poetry Review/Honickman First Book Prize offers publication of a book of poems, a $3,000 award, and distribution by Copper Canyon Press through Consortium. Each year a distinguished poet is chosen to judge the prize and write an introduction to the winning book. The purpose of the prize is to encourage excellence in poetry, and to provide a wide readership for a deserving first book of poems. *River Hymns* is the twentieth book in the series.

WINNERS OF THE AMERICAN POETRY REVIEW/
HONICKMAN FIRST BOOK PRIZE

1998   Joshua Beckman, *Things Are Happening*

1999   Dana Levin, *In the Surgical Theatre*

2000   Anne Marie Macari, *Ivory Cradle*

2001   Ed Pavlić, *Paraph of Bone & Other Kinds of Blue*

2002   Kathleen Ossip, *The Search Engine*

2003   James McCorkle, *Evidences*

2004   Kevin Ducey, *Rhinoceros*

2005   Geoff Bouvier, *Living Room*

2006   David Roderick, *Blue Colonial*

2007   Gregory Pardlo, *Totem*

2008   Matthew Dickman, *All-American Poem*

2009   Laura McKee, *Uttermost Paradise Place*

2010   Melissa Stein, *Rough Honey*

2011   Nathaniel Perry, *Nine Acres*

2012   Tomás Q. Morín, *A Larger Country*

2013   Maria Hummel, *House and Fire*

2014   Katherine Bode-Lang, *The Reformation*

2015   Alicia Jo Rabins, *Divinity School*

2016   Heather Tone, *Likenesses*

2017   Tyree Daye, *River Hymns*

River Hymns

Copyright © 2017 by Tyree Daye. All rights reserved.
Printed in the United States of America. No part of this
book may be used or reproduced in any manner
whatsoever without written permission except in the
case of brief quotations embodied in critical articles and
reviews. Direct all inquiries to: The APR/Honickman
First Book Prize, The American Poetry Review, 320 S.
Broad Street, Hamilton 313, Philadelphia, PA 19102.

Cover photo: Maude Schuyler Clay

Book design and composition: VJB/Scribe

Distribution by Copper Canyon Press/Consortium

Library of Congress Control Number:

ISBN 978-0-9833008-4-7 cloth

ISBN 978-0-9833008-5-4 paper

9 8 7 6 5 4 3 2 FIRST EDITION

River Hymns

Tyree Daye

The American Poetry Review

Philadelphia

For my mother, Joyce Glover;
and for my wife, DeLissa

ACKNOWLEDGMENTS

I would like to thank the editors of the following print and online publications in which these poems, sometimes in different versions, appeared.

At Length: "No Ghost Abandon," "River Goddess Cento," (original title "The River Goddess Speaks") "Tamed"

BOAAT: "In Youngsville"

Four Way Review: "Gin River," "Same Oaks, Same Year"

HeART: "When My Mother had the World on Her Mind, Crickets in Her Ear"

Nashville Review: "For a Kid Death Happens Like This"

The New Engagement: "And we tried to sleep in the summer," "Many Ago," "Southern Silence"

Ploughshares: "Story" (original title "Anything Left")

Forever grateful for Elizabeth Scanlon of American Poetry Review, Gabrielle Calvocoressi and Copper Canyon Press for giving *River Hymns* a spine and a home.

The poem "Prison Poem #2: Or Our Stories in the Key of E" originally appeared in the chapbook *Sea Island Blues* published by Backbone Press.

For support, encouragement, and advice I wish to thank: Dorianne Laux, Joseph Millar, Rob Greene, Eduardo C. Corral, John Balaban, Wilton Barnhart, Vievee Francis, Heather Bowlan, Matthew Wimberley, Dr. Sheila Smith McKoy, Jericho Brown, Toi Derricotte, Cornelius Eady, Evie Shockley, Kevin Young, Lyrae Van Clief-Stefanon, Amber Flora Thomas, Willie Perdomo, Major Jackson, Nicole Sealey, Amanda Johnston, Mahogany L. Browne.

For generous gifts of shelter and sustenance I'm indebted to: North Carolina State University MFA program, Dr. Tracy Ray, The Cave Canem Foundation, William Seraile, Poet House, Nancy Hechinger and others.

Always [Lucille Clifton, Etheridge Knight, Larry Levis]

Contents

Inauaguration

> I come from the clutter of folks
> fixing fish plates in the dead of the dim hour,
> with only a few flood lights lighting faces.
>
> —FROM "SORE"

I am writing this foreword on Martin Luther King Day, 2017. It is four days until we will see our next president inaugurated. I am sitting in the state of North Carolina where I live and where it turns out Tyree Daye lives. I did not know Tyree until I came upon these poems amidst many other remarkable manuscripts. But here we were, living at the same moment in history and living a very few miles apart. In the days after I chose Tyree's manuscript, *River Hymns* for the Honickman, our state of North Carolina underwent what many have referred to as a non-violent coup at the hands of our legislature. As with anything, it depends on who you ask. If you ask me I would say that is accurate. This is all to say, it has been hard to find hope in the world. Thank goodness, then, for Poetry and thank goodness for the poems of Tyree Daye.

When was the last time you experienced something that felt truly new to you? It doesn't have to be poems. It could be some song you heard or some plate of food or the way somebody held you. That feeling of something never felt before that rises like a wave of light right in the center of the body. In one of the darkest times I've ever felt in my life as an American citizen and American poet, I began reading Tyree Daye's manuscript and began to feel that wave of light moving through me. What was it about these poems that felt so different?

I think I first felt it here:

> I'm the doe in my mother's house
> the water covering my hind legs completely
> I drink from the deep end
> of her body
>
> — FROM, "TOWARDS THE MOUTH OF THE RIVER"

or perhaps here

I've only trusted
    four white people in my life
        my mother showed me

the ropes early   I'm afraid
      to untie myself   get down
          from this branch

even the Jesus   on the wall of the church   old and swaying
      has something
          up his sun-touched sleeves

                    —FROM "SOUTHERN SILENCE"

or maybe:

I knew God
was a man

because he put
a baby in Mary

without her
permission.

                    —FROM, "NEUSE RIVER"

What began to build in me as I read these poems was *not* that I had never seen these figures or this landscape before but that I was seeing so much that was familiar to me through an entirely new lens. This seems to me to be important, now more than ever: the ability of the poet to show us a world we thought we knew and then expand our understanding. For instance, I grew up near tobacco fields. I lost my mother. I watched the river where I lived cough up tides of dead fish. And yet. I have not seen any of it quite like Tyree Daye has. And so I become more nuanced in my own vision as I read more deeply into these entirely unique and startling poems. I become a better citizen of the poem, and (I think) the world.

Tyree Daye is a poet of extraordinary ability and surprise. I find new music to delight in every time I come back to this book. I encounter new ways to think about family and community, new ways to wrestle with my own landscape and legacy. Unbeknownst to me a poet named Tyree Daye was writing poems in the same state I was that helped me see my state differently and more deeply. "State" means all sorts of things in that sentence. That's thanks to Tyree's vision, his tremendous gifts. It's an honor to get to welcome this poet's first book into the world.

—Gabrielle Calvocoressi

River Hymns

i.

Dirt Cakes

My Grandmother's body
lives under an ash tree
on an old church ground, her spirit
can be seen making
a maple tree's shadow jealous.

The church's bricks absorb the choir's songs,
they flake Holy Ghost,
If Trouble Don't Come Today.

I visit, fall on my knees, ask
her how she doing? How long
is her hair now?

Does she still like it braided
in front? Still like having
her scalp scratched?
What y'all doing
in heaven today?

She'd tell my mama
don't let a bird get the hair that falls
out your head, they'll use it to build a nest
and you'll never leave Rolesville. Dirt

is the only thing I know that can't die,
it makes sense
we would bury here, makes sense
mama don't want me playing in it.

Lord here

I learned what a bullet does to a back, to a mother.

After every funeral it rains,

     I was told that's God crying in Youngsville.

My uncle walked our holed streets

     until he died sun-soaked, broken in,

left me young boy and bitter in Youngsville.

Hallelujahs knocked on screen doors,

      let the lord in.

     We stood on porches and watched the saved

stitch wings in Youngsville.

Blackberries hung in my aunt's back yard where we cut

     the asshole off a trout,

guts laid on a cutting board in Youngsville.

We were told a storm was a sermon,

     lightning horsewhips the sky,

milks rain in Youngsville.

Tongues

Even the dust that lifted
off the fields had something to say—I listened.
Even the grass spoke.

We turned the woods
behind my house into a playground,

the men that slept there its keepers,
their matted blankets new ground.
A day was measured in how far away
from home we could get.

Our mothers took care of our tongues,
when we only wanted sugar,
Pixy Stix and caramel pieces,
death never stopped wanting,
licked our collarbones like they were covered
in powdered sugar.

Death was never a child, always
had to think of others first.

Before we knew what our bodies were worth
we made wounds the way the sky made blue.

The first time I saw a rabbit
eat its young, I thanked God
for my mother.

Southern Silence

I've only trusted
    four white people in my life
        my mother showed me

the ropes early   I'm afraid
        to untie myself   get down
            from this branch

even the Jesus   on the wall of this church old and swaying
        has something
            up his sun-touched sleeves
tell me the value of my soul
      why he wants it so badly?
           I can't pray

to someone
    who favors
      the men that called us niggers

from their trucks
I touched every part of Thomas Field
                  until I found
the dirt
    I thought could hold me
      what said nothing always grieved

I loved myself
      before I knew
        what I was made of
    so many different things
      will ruin the blood

a bottle of gin   killed three of my uncles

                    one granddaddy

we call it white liquor

        I wanted to cage and bring home

                what I made of myself

look at your proud boy mama

        I wish I only spoke

                in song

made a home

    from these trees

        the way birds do

And We Tried to Sleep in the Summer

my uncle protected me from everything
that wanted me bright and ripened,
the dogs going blood-thick-crazy, matted black fur
        chased kids from house to trailer, we fed

our dog the fat off the back end of the chicken,
        it snarled, trapped me on the porch.

Summer's favorite word was *betta-run,*
we did, prayed for our legs to hold up. The ground
made its own clay coffin,

        lay in any spot
long enough and buzzards would circle,
        dark feathers coiled
            in the day time.
He had to put our dog down, I still hear
the shot now,

my first instructions on death,
left one big patch of red in a green field.
It died the way everyone will,

one minute you're alive, the next you are
the empty bedroom us kids are afraid to go in.

Summer dried all the blood in my uncle's heart,
left it broken and swollen
        in his olive-colored sleep.

Caged

place the turtle in the mouth
                of the barrel
watch its darkness swallow
this is the first time you realize

how a body can be used
for others' gain

others' nourishment
this is how you make stew
your uncle says

first fatten   last kill

boil then simmer
the same way you do a rabbit's small frame

my uncle grabbed a white tail
                by its hind legs

stuffed it in a long box
they went for 20 a head

never sell the mamas
keep the stock growing

keep 'em fed
the turtle's water clean

she's the queen of the cage
one turtle could feed

the whole family
know the price of meat

a sick hen when you see one

Wade Through

my mama dreamed
belly dancers dressed in red
around a buffed coffin
then her sister a *slick-haired woman*
was gone

no one heard the hush fire
in the kitchen

my mama grew up in a tin roof house
near a field of peaches
green arrow-shaped leaves washed
      then covered to suck fever out

her mama told her if you see a hummingbird
      yellow and blue wind
      under a small head
      someone's going to die
someone always did

her daddy on a small wooden bedframe
      its brown fading gray

ash in dreams favor stars
      my mama is afraid she'll dream me dead

when it rains she tells me to keep my head down
it only takes a drop of water to drown you

I visit her on weekends
      bring flowers she places in a vase

wings still in her ears
lilies on the table white as a skull

River Goddess Cento

Coal laughs at ashes not knowing its fate.

You are not like a child

who when carried only presses on my back,

you press on every part of my body.

He has been shown to the dead.

Nobody can say they've settled

anywhere forever, it is only the mountains

which do not move. What escapes a prairie fire?

What will your hands look like if we meet after

you have gone around the mountain?

Greens

His heart was broken,
like an empty gin bottle.
In the end he was drinking himself into it.

But I don't know.
I was six and still fooled
by the light on the river when he died,

decided not to ask my mother
about her favorite brother.
Some curled years later

night mothers me,
a tit full of beer at my side,
a shadow with large veins smiling
against the wall.

Lately I can't handle tears
or too much salt in my greens.

He died in his sleep, the way a crop of tobacco,
one night healthy, full of purple flowers, the next
shrunken in the overnight rain.

Strike the Stone See if it's Thinking of Water

A belt taken to my legs

        because I flooded her ears

with every sin I heard my drunk uncles say.

At seven I wanted to be a blue and red parrot

        in an old jungle
           tree.

I repeated words like *love*   *baby*   *little*

heart. Strike the stone until it hollers. Teach it water,

she was taught. Death happens in tides and trickles,

near the wet mouth where everything finally meets.

O Jesus, I could be a mule or plow the furrows with my hands
                if need be.

O my sweet Jesus what kind of cross is that? Rub the stone,

what it leaves on your thumb is a letter unopened.

A beat-en from my mother

        was how I learned that my mouth could be a coffin.

The way God teaches with a storm dividing a field,

        a child face down in the flooding.

Sore

His hand-built garage, wired for AC, scattered
with rusty hammers, broken John Deere parts,
a dance floor made out of scrap plywood
under the *Taylorville* sign, a barrel
where the empties go.

Saturday nights were for forgetting
the way your boss calls you *boy*, *gal*,
for splitting a fifth of gin, a 24-pack of Budweiser,
aunts and uncles, friends of the family,
ex's, husbands and wives all drunk,
a cheap smile spread across their mouths.

My aunt's slow gallop to an offbeat tempo
looks like a flowering tobacco field,
purple humming the night dark. This is a ritual
of aching legs, sore backs, why the body
wants to stay young. I try to tell myself
the days don't connect tissue to bone.
When the devil was shaking the dance floor,
every swirl, lock, pop looked like worship,
like work, tilling the ground near a magnolia tree,
several heads of cabbage,
seeds in the ridges of their soles.

I come from a clutter of folks
fixing fish plates in the dead of the dim hour,
with only a few flood lights lighting faces.

Everyone here has picked tobacco,
or their mama or daddy has,

gummed, they saw green
in their sharecropper's sleep
and believed that the night made the river sigh.
A blackbird flew into our little house once
and my grandmother died the next week.

I'm still too young to know what *inherited* means,
a few years from sneaking beer with cousins
near the big muscle of a river,
our hands soft and ordinary, unbruised.

Gin River

If the Neuse River was gin
we would've drunk to its bottom,

       its two-million-year-old currents alive
       with shad, sunfish, redhorse, yellow lance,

all the blood from the Tuscarora War.

We would have drunk it all,
       aunts and uncles would have led us in Big Bill Broonzy's
       "When I Been Drinking,"

until everything inside us began to dance
and we all joined in,

silt around our ankles,
our footprints on the banks
leading down to the water.

Street Birds

We hunt here, I was shown death
at the age of seven, something dead
in my uncle's hands.

I touched the belly of the black snake
felt its body a muscle tense.

I know nothing
        of the baby birds cut
from the sour smell of its stomach,

just as I know nothing
        of the sister and brother I watched cut
from the back seat of a flipped over car,
their own little cave.

My uncle tossed the thin-winged birds
into the air, lost
in the overgrown wood forever.

They never flew, never rode
their Huffy bikes from street end
                        to street end.

Never raced each other,
never turned a bike into a motorcycle
with an empty orange soda can. The black snake tail

will swirl until the sun goes down,
until the devil comes to get it.

I began to pray
for a new skin for my mother.

Once I could name
     all the new things.
Mutt puppies, new heads of lettuce,
my uncle's new car, new red heart.

When My Mother Had the World on Her Mind, Crickets in Her Ear

1. Boy, don't let a shadow in you, I never want to see the devil in your eyes, a traceable line of your daddy's.
2. If you dream about fish or a river, somebody's pregnant, we need the water more than it needs us.
3. Dream about snakes, you haven't been living right, wash your hands of it.
4. They're shooting boys who look like you. You know my number, use it, keep all your blood.
5. Stay
6. alive.

Pray to the River Goddess

We held hands in the kitchen,
made a black moon, the mouth of a barrel,
what burned in it blistered in us,
          praying for nourishment
is to hope the juice from the greens
cures my uncle's cold,
helps the ache in my aunt's back.

The way she bends as if always giving thanks
for minimum wage.

To say *nourishment* is to say *mercy*.
To say *mercy* is to say *amen, amen, amen*.

And if the body is a church
          in my mother's house
then praise be the maze of her eyes
as she stomps her foot with an aunt's *thank you*.
And if the body is a church in the river, then let the water
drown these worshipers. If the tongue be a preacher,
taste buds the holy ghost, let it speak from the gut
to the pulpit of the mouth.

Every hallelujah in this circle
is endless.
To say *hallelujah*
          is to say *we still here,*
I won't let the water turn we away.

In the house of my mother
stand three generations
causing a tide.

Blues for June Bug: Told in the Key of B

they found him face down
    in field of cabbage
good dirt in his mouth

his thick hair its own rain catcher
on his uncombed head

he could fool any yellow-spotted trout
to bite on his thin line

knew that to talk to the water
    you needed a horse's face

that the sky rewrote the river's mood
he could grow anything
could raise a garden by lifting his hands

received calls from miles around
save my tomatoes help my squash
can you do anything about these mites?

we planted him in that same field
his mama and daddy was

together they grew purple tobacco flowers

God must have had some greens
in heaven that were wilting
around the edges

Neuse River

Tell them not to go
to the banks alone.

Tell them where
they can drink

without watching
over their shoulders.

Tell them drowning
is third on your list

of concerns.
First is *lie down*,

second, *come here*.
Even the water

I was baptized in
isn't safe.

I knew God
was a man

because he put
a baby in Mary

without her
permission.

Towards the Mouth of the River

triangles of blue on my face:
the fins of a salmon dying between
two rocks

~

light is my grandmother
closing her hands
pleading in air
    thicker near the water

~

I'm a doe in my mother's house
the water covering my hind legs completely
    I drink from the deep end
of her body

~

I turn back into a river when I leave
step onto the porch
flood the yard
water never forgets
it's water

~

whirling disease causes
some trout to chase their own tails
before they die

the fish disappearing
into little orange orbs

—

I'm circling this graveyard afraid
to walk the gravel road between the stones

—

I tell the light
       of summers it left me quiet
holding a wound under a rusted faucet

—

light has never been light

—

my grandmother left this soybean-field-
covered-town with an infection
     I had as a child
held down
a plastic tube funneled in   thick pus sucked
from my ear

—

a tooth pulled from a 13-years-old boy's left foot
the dead wait in the oddest places

—

what is God but rain spilling me over?

—

salmon rely on the moon
to find the waters where they were born
        the light on the Neuse River firm

—

the moon also points

—

I put enough dope up my nose to bury
any dead folk hiding in my head

—

my body one big draining
        one big body of brown water

—

If I get clean
the fish come back to life   un-die

Same Oaks, Same Year

My cousin kept me and his little brother
saved me from our uncle's

pit bull, then spent seven years
in prison for his set.

Every other word
he said was *blood.*

⁓

Uncle Nuggie showed us
          how to make a BB rattle
inside a squirrel.

Two small holes,
enter and exit.

All summer I wondered
what leaves the body?

ii.

The Name I Carry

Mama, your shadow on the wall
is still crying, your mother told me
your shadow doesn't recognize the lines
                   on my hands,

that your shadow is what the sun touches,
what's blazed always stomped out.
Daddy your shadow's heart beat
is always asking about itself.

How many times must I tell it that it's a man on fire?

What a price
      I have on my head.

What a name I carry.

You are your daddy's son.

The way me and my brother, his legs over
my shoulders, make one big shadow
                  in the yard,
make one big father.

Story

I'd hear a sound off in the trees
and follow it for hours.
I touched the bark of an old maple and watched
the ants take my hand, those tiny legs
on the flesh like gripping a ghost's hand.

Mama still
in the front yard cleaning
trout, like her life there is the gutting,
the clipping of blue fins.

Once I sliced my leg open on the fence leading
to this wildness, two rivers poured out of me.
The Neuse, Haw, every fish dead,
the ground wouldn't take all the blood.

The waters of my mama's life
are not my own. She raised me
out of black snakes and Clorox
to get the ticks off, Clorox
to get the dirt out.

Mama you couldn't have had anything left
to love yourself with after loving me,
men down here mixed blood with water
and called it wine.

We all had to kiss the devil in the mouth,
spit like the cinnamon candies
from my aunt's summer purse.
We live in the same house your mama died in,
we talk with her ghost as if she still had a tongue.

Tamed

I was the unbroken horse
of that town, slept standing up,
held on to the breeze like wildflowers.

I kept caterpillars in jars,
my mama let them go,
I figured they just disappeared.

There are moments you can hear God
say things soft-spoken, the sun
settling between thin pines.

Collected crickets in 2 liter bottles,
dropped them on a path far from the house
one or two at the bottom drowning
in the last swig of cola, the smell of mama's
leaf pile faint and almost gone.

My mama would say
to kill a cricket
is a sin against the night.

River Hymns

Mother let light be all of you and nothing of me.

I will always be a junkie you know that,

always want to kill the mule stomping in my head.
Do you remember days I refused to be awakened?

Dirt cakes gin rivers burn the roof of my mouth,
the world *bright bone white* on your mind,
crickets in the hollow of your ears,

you know the one bird still singing
in this late October is your brother,

even with wings he sounds like Sam Cooke.

Blow kisses to cardinals
because they're good luck you said,
you sang the uneven blues for June Bug
his bloomed body off behind the trees,

his last sermon went dear body
dear mother I tried to sleep
in the summer and failed.

Hurricane Floyd conjured your mother
from swept up dust no ghost abandoned
the egg white sky of Youngsville,

because of you I'm addicted
to learning every Whitney
song.

Oh lady of the river thank you,

my water birth river mouth
for the blue stroked birds
               you renamed.

Learning Whitney

My father loved my mama
quiet. She never was.

Sang as she dusted,
Whitney was her back-up singer.

He'd disappear, stumble in,
bright blues still in his mouth.

I come from a family of men
who thought saying I love you

was something you saved for sleep or the dead
and tears could get your ass whooped.

Blooming

For Dorianne

Do you remember
that November I was losing weight

and writing poems that had no hope,
no way of coming out of poverty?

You saw what little light I held
between my dying teeth,

I thought was only a meal
leftover from too late in the day.

Remember Birds

We were never allowed to say lucky,
who needs a genie
when you have God?

When the water rises
all the birds disappear,
we prepare our homes for the flood,

the way a preacher prepares a body,
hands at your side
or over your chest.

Everyone gathered somewhere to pray.
No one questions
who God will take,

someone is always taken.
Remember cardinals are good luck
but never touch a lone red feather
being held by grass blades.

My mama used to say,
boy you better make sure
they make me look good for the lord.

For a Kid Death Happens Like This

Your mother is not watching
Young and the Restless,
but sits in the quiet, dark living room.
She won't care that your bed
has gone unmade for three days,
sheets in a sour ball in the corner,
the carton of milk round
as your cousin's belly.

Outside you place
your ear to the ground,
hear the ants marching
to a cadence of *the dead, the dead*
but to them it sounds like sugar.
If anyone ever catches you
near the two liquor houses
that almost touch like second cousins,
your mother will beat you sky color.

Suddenly like rain
your father arrives.
Takes you outside
in the gravel driveway
to look under the hood
of his green truck.
You stare at the bones
of his wrist, his nose snub
like yours. He asks you to pass
the tool, says that's a flat head
not a Phillips.

The cancer in your grandmother's kidneys
never whispered. It grabbed the mic
and started yelling *the dead, the dead,*
a deacon for dialysis, for insulin, for water.
You remember them all around her bed.
Your mother, your father's sister
you barely knew, the father
you wanted like your littlest cousin
wanted ponies with blond hair.

Prison Poem #2: Or Our Stories in the Key of E

I never understood your love
for the color red. Until she walked to the door
turned around and asked would I be okay.
Even the moon behind her is leaving.

My mother keeps reminding me
that poverty and booze don't mix
and can kill any man.
I wanted to send you poems
to cover all the gray surrounding you,
but I never did.

What do we do with all these stories
of pond fish and dog fighting,
getting caught smoking behind the shed,
me hiding by the pond, everyone thinking
I fell in? Learning that crack smells
like burning oil from our uncle's Chevy,
that the summer heat
and a woman that doesn't love you
can bust a man's heart?

Fire Water

I sat in the dark house
      used lightning for light

a storm speaks every language

the devil was never there
when I needed him
you can pour gasoline over the river
and watch it burn

                              the river fuels only on itself
boil the water before you drink it
        mercy was the first medicine
no prayer I give you will end

put uncle's bones down
we buried him in a gray suit
it rained all that day

water buried itself
gone in the morning
dirt is also a womb

aunt's fire worship   *mercy*
is cheap gin

someone open the stove
      it's cold in this house

I can see the ghost inside me
        my dreams have songs

I know I'm dreaming of my grandmother
                    when my mother is sitting cross-legged

on the porch
the flowers on her purple dress
            a year across her shoulders
and is singing

Speak Lord/speak to me

Am I dreaming or conjuring?
                    I couldn't tell you

put uncle's hats in the closet
keep its door closed

                    no amen will *have mercy*
am I praying or am I conjuring?
            I couldn't tell you

        where to lay these bones
but in the fire my aunts made to keep us warm
I'll die to keep a bullet out of your back
                I am praying
                        Lord what do you do
        with these words?
thick   begging   wings

bury them in my uncle's tomb of a garage
                isn't a hammer a bent,
        unfinished cross?

isn't trying to start a lawnmower
an act of worship?

    its motor speaking in tongues

In His Mouth

I am my daddy's scored hands

each line something that began and ended

he let go of my useless fingers

I am his poked mouth saying I love you

I am a tongue

      behind in his teeth

my mother saw me

      drowning in his mouth

laid down under him

saw me closer   they kissed

I entered   an idea

said *I love you*

I was given a name

Rock-a-bye

If I made a map of me
             my mother's body would appear
                          her map makes mine

on my arrival into breath

             into her softness

I stole the little light
             my mother had left

I've smoked enough cigarettes

             to keep up with every train

in this never-bloomed town

this town
             all dead and birdsong

even now as I am heading to a city
             she's never been

her body
             is a never-watered dandelion

even now I'm thinking of her fingers
                          wrapped around my own

             cradled
             cradled

how can I tell her *I love you*

in a way she hasn't heard my father say before

Whitney Houston Cento

For my Mother

Streets seem so empty
now, can't stop to think
about my life here today.

What if I'd never met you,
where would I be right now.

A song still unsung.

Nobody loves me like you do.

Is it Love

I was made to wrestle a cousin
in the middle of the living room,

the small brown floral sofa and chairs
pushed against the wall.

Two older cousins over us drunk,
the television must have been broken

or someone asked if there was fight on.
Then one of them looked at us.

I'm in the same house my grandmother
died in. We don't own this house, never will.

Our landlord white and old
comes over smiling.

I wonder where he lives.
Why my mother cusses him,

gets him in, out. We own kerosene heaters,
the dust on our faces as we tried to prove something

we couldn't tie down to the floor,
throw love at the wall, see if it hollers.

Planet Theory

It scares me to think
once the moon wasn't there.
That it's nothing but debris.
I galloped twelve miles in leftover snow and footprints
because a friend said he would give me a cigarette,
all I had was my stolen flask,
the time you said *I don't love you anymore*
and I walked to the library in the rain
to find books on depression.
The hunger I had when I didn't
want to ask you for food
because my pride slept
where my hunger was muscled over
by smoke
My leftover loves.
My fuck the man, sleep all day.
My Uncle Boo Boo gripping
a rifle in our back yard,
the rabies running through
our dog's body like the gin in his.
My mother's mouth. My good times
in a plastic bag. The things we do for money.
My father's nose.
Some broken things.
The brother I haven't spoken to.

Last night I named the moon *Glitter*
after the first stripper to wrap
her legs around my own
and blow smoke in my face.

Her dance faded like anyone's smoke
once all the blue starts dying
as any day's blue does.

Dear God

What I pray for
is what scares me the most,

my brother's body
shrunken into an October morning.

I watched him
bury his eyes in the hospital walls
white as Jesus' face,
even his praying was sickly.

My father re-learning me
what absence means,
how bastard sounds on the tongue.

I call this a love poem
so I don't place any negativity
into the world,

love poem, love poem, love
poem.

A List of Waters

1.

The scar that flows from my aunt's thigh
to the boulder of her swollen ankle is a map
of the Haw River,
each toe a Blue Heron.

2.

My mama's water
        is all water, I'm every river rock
inside her being smoothed over.

3.

The palms of my uncle's hands
are the Deep River when he is holding a gutted trout.

Always something
is bleeding.

4.

You saw her bloody
and did nothing,
you Yellow Perch.

5.

My uncles sinned openly
on Sunday,
fed in the daytime,
      a White Catfish.

6.

My smallest cousin is a salamander in their father's
      Neuse River arms, legs hanging there
like Blackwater.

7.

Every woman
who has ever told me to clean my face
is the Atlantic Ocean.

8.

The shoreline of this beach
is also a history lesson,
these sea shells
have blood on them.

9.

I dream mostly in floods.

Dear Children

Today I am the same age, same song that played when my mother had me.

I'm side B of my father's record, hopefully you understand

jazz by now. The first time you hear me

and your great uncle talking in the kitchen,

remember he was a singer,

Sam Cooke was his favorite. Never get into conversation

        about love

with him, he'll break your heart.

If you follow the dead long enough,

you'll start to confuse their voices

with the wind stuck in these tall pines.

What I am trying to ring

        from my dirt-tasting-tongue

is that you can let go of her dress hem now.

Today I'm my mother pushing you out beneath

some trees, you are a river leaving my body.

Glowing

Always catch the flame,
pace the woods,
gather the dead
trees, you want the branches
to crack when you bend them.
Some good rocks
to hold the burning.
The burning to hold
the light, the light
to hold   the dark,
everything cupped in hands. To hold

a gin bottle and cut lose my tongue,
that's what these nights are for.

Let it sit pink
and glowing by the fire
it only speaks
of what's left behind.

Tonight I tell God
that even when I beg,
don't give me another mother,
I can't handle a wake twice.

With the living/With the light

autumn and you're you again

        one thing God gave us

the skill to even when dead

      look good

    mercy
in a house filled with the living
I miss you the most

these are how I spend my days
looking over a tobacco field
swollen with light
your ghost
repeats the phrase
burn it all down
      a fire in your singing
you from where the soybeans fields
learn black backs the hard way
      I hear *mercy*
in the leaves breaking under my feet

I'm rewriting every conversation overheard
in my mother's kitchen until I find you
between the gossip

How Long Is Her Hair Now?

We still celebrate
my Grandmother's birthday
by frying a slab of fish,
smothering a flounder
in Texas Pete,
chicken in Sweet Baby Ray's,
someone puts on Marvin,
someone says I love you.

How can we lift enough
smoke to reach you?
Our cookout has the blues,
I can't tell you why
I walk old country roads
looking for your spirit.

I hear you speaking
near the river,
where the water
slows against rocks.

My mother says
the best thing to do
is get addicted to God.

But I write from inside my body,
what's the price of being
obsessed with the dead?
No ghost abandoned,
you mostly
speak of wind.

Someone put on Marvin,
someone say I love you.

In my purple bedroom,
I've heard a woman
long dead speak of gardens,
tomatoes, squash,
white tobacco flowers, *lilies*
are pretty, but they are weeds.

By the elementary school
we used to pick sweet potatoes,
played games like
that's my car,
that's my house.

The land murmurs
in our hands,
where to grow
the biggest melons,

the place where June Bug
finally died,
what's so sweet
must be sacred.

We mended the horses
rubbed an old muzzle
until it was time.

I can still see your silhouette
in the window like a kiss
to a father long gone.

What do you think
when you see my loneliness?
Living ghost? I must learn
the language of rain
to speak to plants
how a seed
turns to flower, a Genesis
in each pot.

In the kitchen
I haven't stepped in today,
I can hear you
among the spoons
and butter knives
in the drawer.

What Is God but Rain Spilling Me Over?

My mother's name made

too-tight-a-space in my mouth, until I knew

    I was saying many names, how the dead keep waiting

for me to say enter, two generations moved twice inside me.

    My mother says letting go means removing the dead that won't play ghost.

But I can't, they're the rocks in my liver, cleaning me. Enter I tell them.

In the morning I pull a tendon out of my throat

leave it in the bathroom sink curled, it belongs to a great aunt,

    she died making a fist.

My uncle sleeps on my artery, sings Sam Cooke to its knock.

Victor lays his head on my feet, his back no longer bloody,

reminds them of walking all over Youngsville,

smoking cigarettes behind the school, running from red coat dogs.

Maybe the dead also gather near the river to drink and confess

in the ribcage of pines. *It feels good to not have blood* one says,

I miss what touching water feels like, I can't bear

the weight of what beginning again means.

Sam Cooke Cento

for Uncle Boo Boo

Thought we said goodbye last night
but you're here to stay.
You old gloomy sight
wish I forget you

stop haunting me now.

You're the one
who knows me well.
Might as well get used to you.

Good morning heartache
sit down.

June Bug's Last Sermon

I haven't heard silence in a while,

even what is not said

has a mouth, pink tongue,

city gettin' closer to the river,

I hear it moanin' way into the night,

street lamps tryin' to compete with stars.

The moon dipped, returned to God,

I'm a man that goes around

collectin' seeds, so when the melons bud,

I know every hair on its stem.

I'm my daddy's first good thing,

my mama all water,

both made ghost last winter,

buried them in their own lonesome valley,

I hope to die by own hands.

Dust, dust and ashes.

This body down.

Say River, See River

I threw up the river last night

trout already gutted   salamanders rocking

between the books on my bedroom floor
then the river stood up   bowlegged it walked

like it was drunk   like it was an uncle

so I followed the dizzy river
into my mother's backyard

watched it fall and flood the houses

pick itself up   laugh it off

we splashed past where the men

slept on the ground their low eyes always

where they laid at night   I wondered
if they counted the stars together

until it turned into a Lightnin' Hopkins' song
21 22 *my black dog blues*

if they played Spades for planets
toasted Wild Irish Rose to the Seven Sisters

the river took me to a big graveyard
we didn't cut through

funneled around
ran a damp finger along the fence

the river would catch a name as we passed the straight stones
and every so often say one

        Philips   *Jones*

the dead heard the wet voice
and started calling back *River*

Notes

"Strike the Stone see if it's Thinking of Water" title is burrowed from Rita Dove's poem "In the Bulrush" and burrows language from *Sula* by Toni Morrison.

"River Goddess Cento" actual lines from *Masai, Myths, Tales and Riddles* by A.C Hollis.

"Whitney Houston Cento" actual lines by Whitney Houston.

"Sam Cooke Cento" actual lines by Sam Cooke.

About the Author

Tyree Daye is a Cave Canem fellow from Youngsville, North Carolina. He received his MFA in poetry from North Carolina State University. Daye's work has been published in *Prairie Schooner, Nashville Review, Four Way Review,* and *Ploughshares.* Daye recently won the Amy Clampitt Residency for 2018 and The Glenna Luschei Prairie Schooner Award for his poems in the Fall 2015 issue.